For Buzz —

Ric Masten

1/12/05

stark naked

By the same author

A THIN BODY OF WORK
SUNFLOWERS
LET IT BE A DANCE
SPEAKING POEMS
HIS & HERS
THE VOICE OF THE HIVE